AF351622

WARNING!

Lots of crazy words!

© Matthew Hitch &
  Sunok Moon 2023

Author: Matthew Hitch

Co-author: Sunok Moon

Illustrator: Matthew Hitch

Cover Design: Brittany Hitch

Layout Design: Matthew Hitch

Text Design: Matthew Hitch

Image Manager: Matthew Hitch

~~Vain Meglomaniac: Matthew Hitch~~

Credits Editor: Matthew Hitch

Image Manager Manager: S. Moon

Image Manager Manager Control: Absolutely no one

Artistic Arguer: Sunok Moon

Dishwasher: Matthew Hitch (occasionally Sunok Moon)

Title: Captain Matt's Super Crazy Fun

Big Kid Phonics 4 Student Book

ISBN 979-11-93590-28-7

First published 2023

Published by Hitch Publishing

info@supercrazyfun.net

All rights reserved. No part of this publication may be reproduced, stored in a retrieval system, or transmitted, in any form or by any means, without the prior permission of the copyright holders, with the exception of small excerpts for review purposes or promotion of the contents or characters. This exception excludes any publication containing sexually explicit content, or content that may be perceived as "obscene."

This textbook came about as the result of 20 years of trying to make kids enjoy learning English. It is designed around the use of the rhotic R and other characteristics of English pronunciation common in North America. We believe it can be used in other parts of the world as most phonics books can, and we are keen to hear feedback from anyone who tries this.

We want to make clear that the word "crazy" used in the title is in relation to any of the common definitions illustrated below, and does not refer in any way to the meaning "insane."

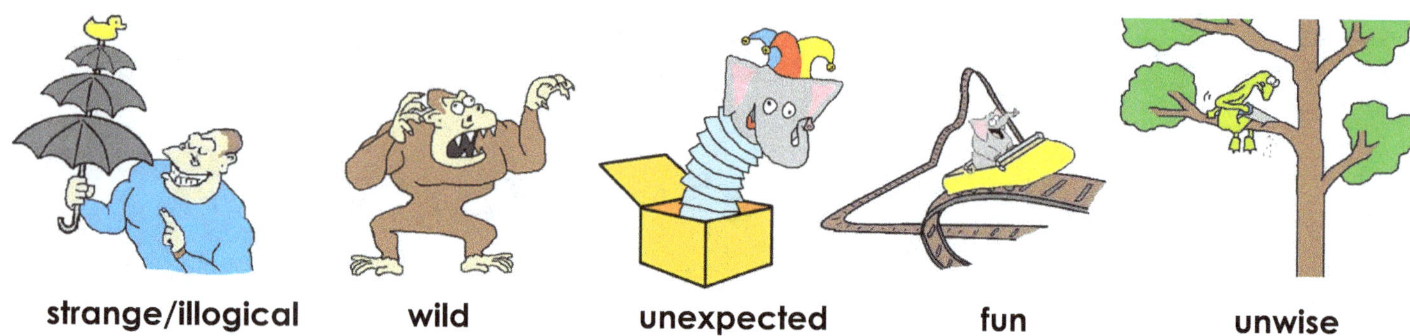

strange/illogical   **wild**   **unexpected**   **fun**   **unwise**

About the Authors:

Matthew Hitch has taught English in Korea for the better part of 20 years and holds a master's degree in applied linguistics. He clearly does not have a pig nose, and by most accounts is not at all malodorous. He also cuts a dashing figure according to his wife.

Sunok Moon prefers to go by the name Michelle, and is in fact quite scary as reported in the bio on the back of this book. She has a degree in English literature and has taught English in Korea for approximately 3 weeks longer than Matthew, who is writing this and finds it weird to refer to himself in the third person.

Contents

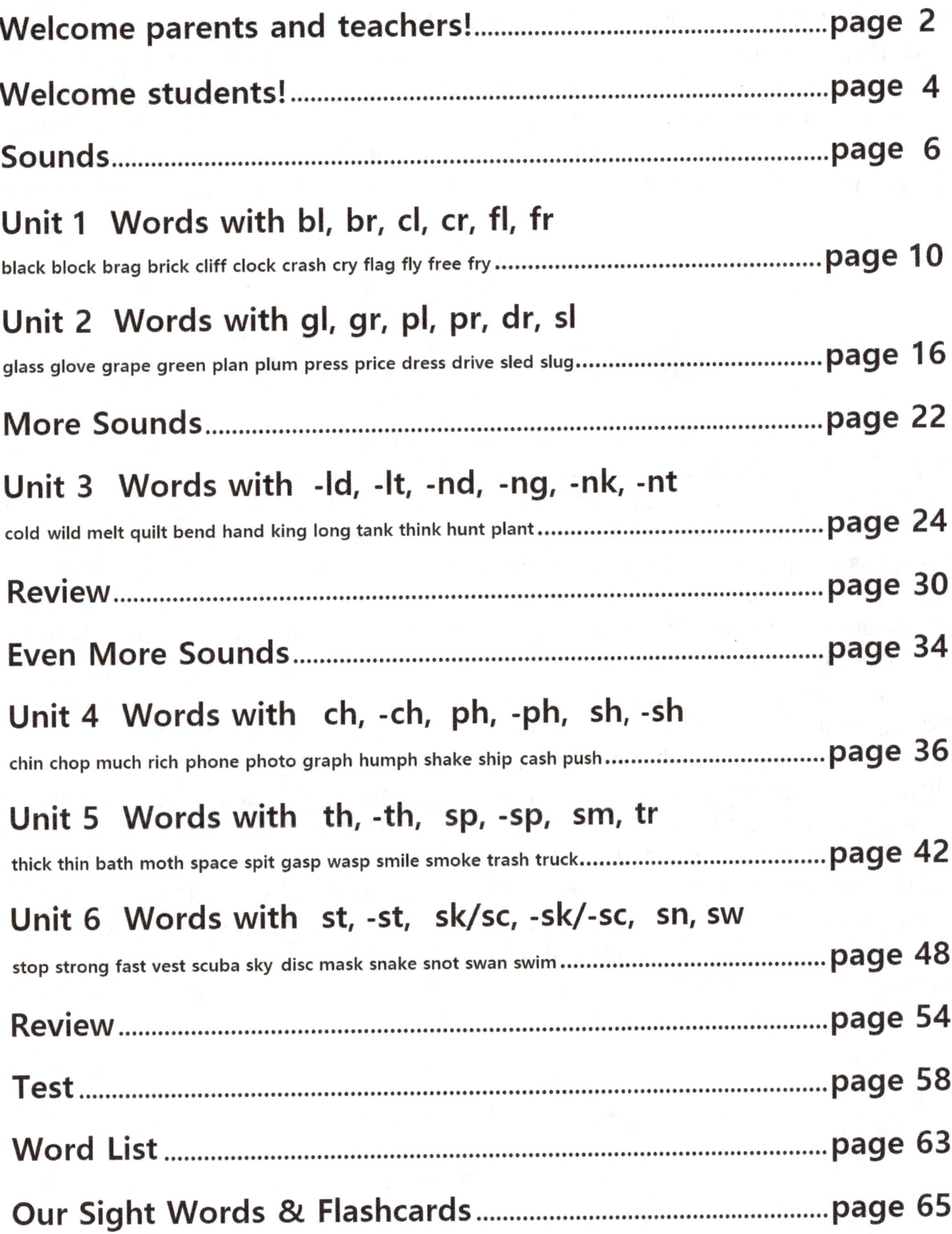

Welcome parents and teachers!

Thank you for considering our book. Phonics books are notoriously boring, so this is the last bastion of publishing where even the tiniest bit of creativity can raise the bar (sorry phonics book publishers, but it's true). With that said, we humbly offer you our content. We have also intentionally challenged convention in a few ways. Much of what we have to say may be used or discarded though, and these books can be used just like any other mainstream phonics book. We hope you will choose to use whatever you please and dispose of the rest.

Please allow us to explain just where our method of teaching phonics may diverge from mainstream approaches, and please do forgive us for sharing information from what is undeniably the most mind-numbingly boring and seemingly useless field of study, linguistics. Most phonics books are not written by scholars in the field of linguistics. They are mostly written by early childhood educators, so perhaps that's the first divergence. We'll start with how we sound out consonants. In linguistic studies it is not uncommon for consonants to be distinguished by using a vowel (usually "ah") on both sides. This means a "V" sounds like "ahvah" and an "F" sounds like "ahfah" and so on. Most phonics books distinguish consonant sounds without such preceding vowel, but they do follow with a vowel in the form of the schwa. This is fine for most consonants, but the ones that are able to be maintained until breath is exhausted can be confusing with a schwa where they end a word. It's mostly ESL students who feel this confusion, but we think it doesn't hurt to teach those consonants without a schwa to native speakers as well, so where "V" sounds like "və" in most phonics books, in our book it is presented as "vvvvvvv" with no schwa. We apply this to all long consonant sounds in our audio files (L,M,N&R are also presented as long with a tiny schwa sound at the end though). If you have read this far, we take our hats off to you. Most would be fast asleep by now.

The next divergence is our use of Magic E. We chose Magic E for the fun potential. The Split Digraphs just can't seem to hold a crowd. Magic E is no longer used in most educational settings for many reasons, but mostly because as a rule it cannot be defined clearly. We do mention that split digraphs are better though, mainly to extend an olive branch to all the teachers we hope will buy our books.

And the final divergence we would like to mention is our choice of words. Our choice of words may seem a bit odd at times throughout the books, but we chose them for their potential for keeping kids engaged over their usefulness. We approach a phonics book as a tool to teach about sounds much more than vocabulary. Poop, vomit, spit, fart, snot, and burp are the most popular with our students. We tried to find a spot for booger, but alas...

Our word choice is also strange in that it includes words that have the long E vowel when teaching split digraphs. Most phonics books glance over the long E vowel. The argument we have heard for this is that it is difficult for the younger students, but we suspect that it's avoided more because it's difficult for authors to find suitable words. We decided to give it a try, and our experience is that the long E words we chose are not that difficult for our students to grasp. Given that English is their second language, we believe native English speaking kids will cope with them just fine. Also you may notice our sight words are not all actually sight words - oops! Anyway, we hope you enjoy our silly books.

Welcome students!

Now we will learn
how to "blend"
sounds!
Blend means "mix
together."

But we don't actually put them
in a blender!
It's more like we let them go
down the waterslide together.

There is no room between blended sounds. The have to squeeze tightly together.

Consonant blends have to be more than one, but not more than six.

It seems a bit unfair, doesn't it?

English has a lot of rules that seem unfair.

Let's get started...

Welcome Students!   5

Sounds

Vowels

There are two kinds of letters. The 5 letters below are called "vowels." The rest of the alphabet are called "consonants."

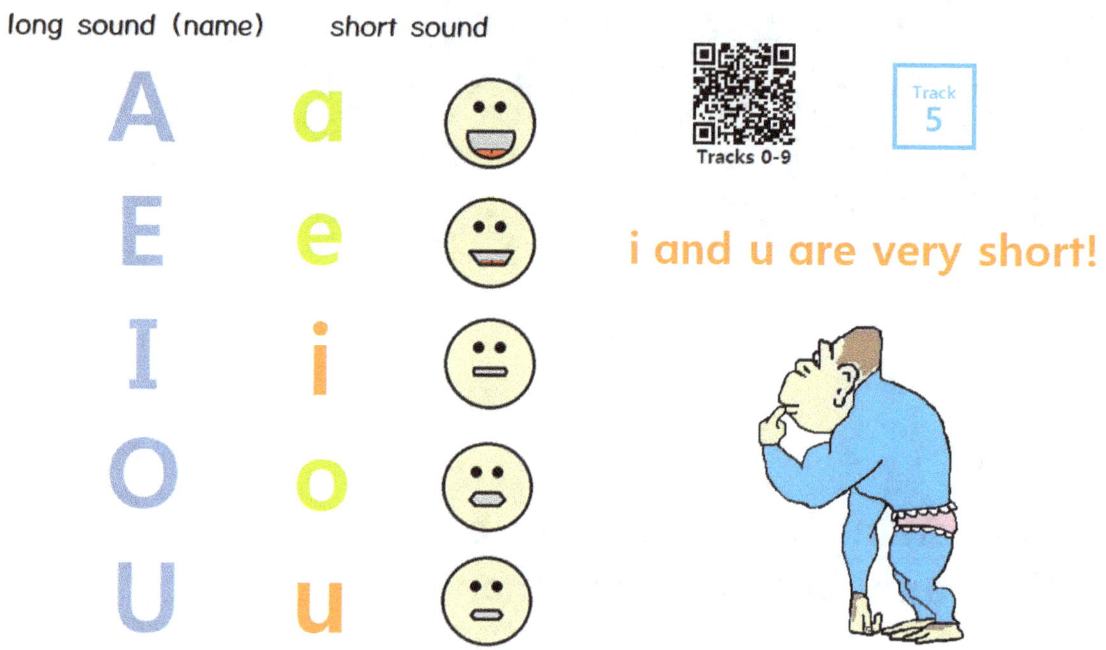

Some vowels can make a blend too, but let's talk about them in the next book!

From here this book is just about consonants.

Digraphs

Remember that group that soften their sounds around h? They're a bit like blends, but they just make one new sound, except for W.

W didn't want to be in that group anymore because wh can't end words.

They have new friends now. Can you guess what they all have in commmon?

Sounds

Voiced and unvoiced sounds

So if we take wh out, all the softened pairs have no voice at all, right?

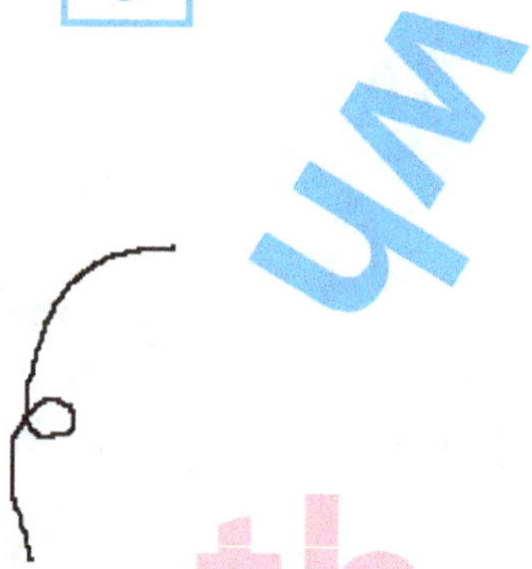

sh ch ph th

Well, not quite. Th is sometimes voiced.

Sometimes voiced

th:

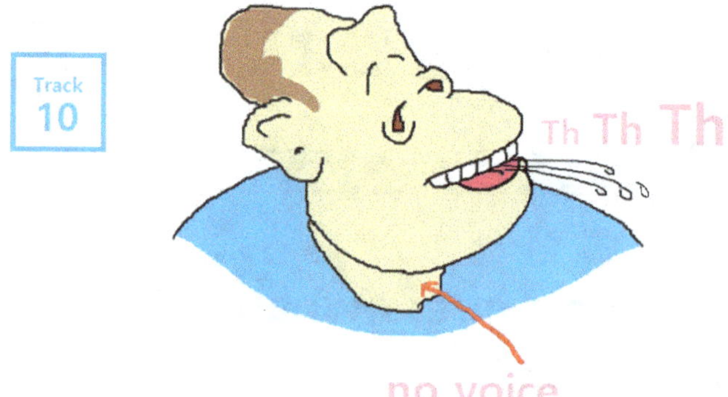

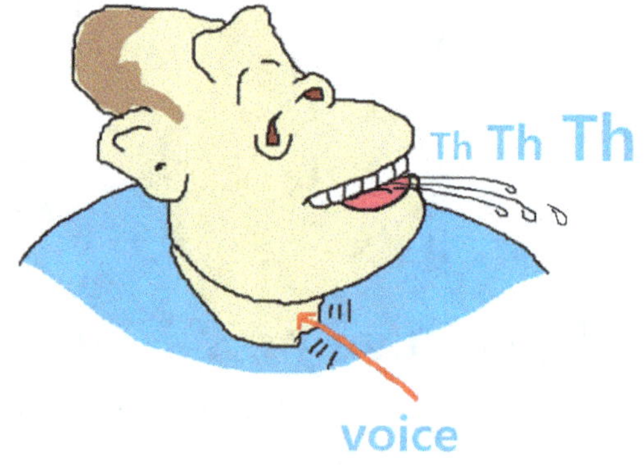

S is voiced sometimes too, but Z doesn't like it at all.

Sounds

Y is a spy!

Y seems like a good consonant.   **But Y really wants to be a vowel.**

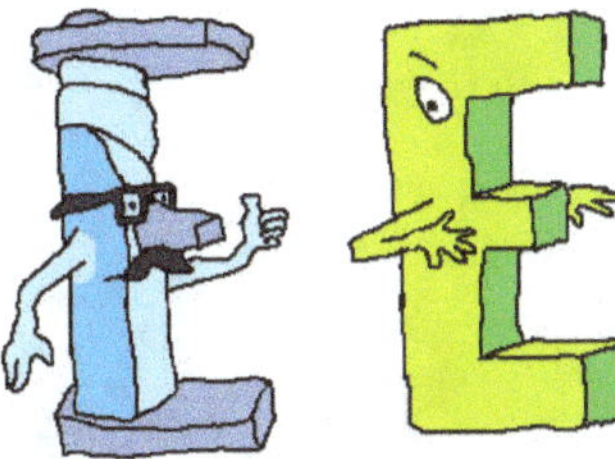

Y likes being an I.   **Or even the long E sound!**

**So in a blend, Y prefers
to sound like a vowel.**   **Perhaps you can hear when
Y is being a vowel.**

Double Consonants

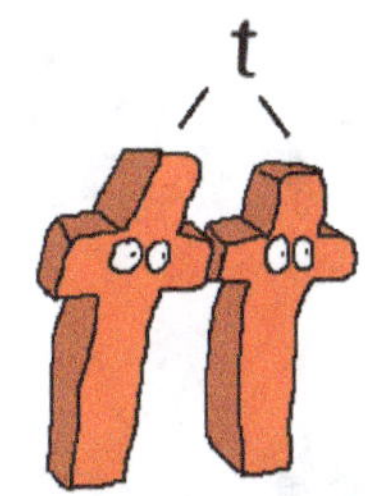
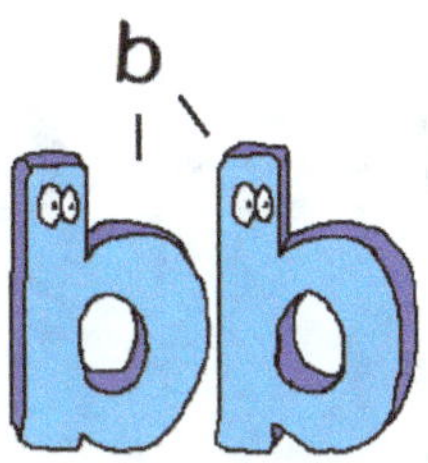

**Double consonants are easy to understand. They just make
the same sound at the same time. And "ck" are like that too.**

Listen, point, and make the sound:  Words with **bl br cl cr fl fr**

Tracks 10-19

Track 14

1   b + l   =   bl

2   c + r   =   cr

3   f + l   =   fl

Listen, point, and say the word: Track 15

1   bl + ock = block   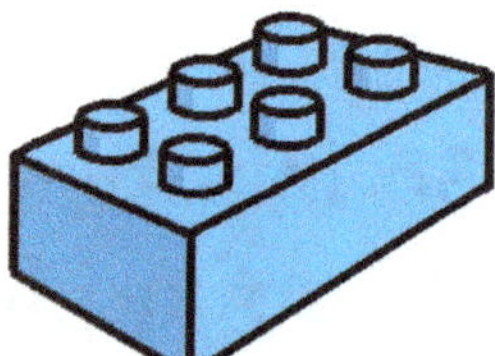

2   cr + ash = crash   

3   fl + ag = flag   

Follow the rules

1 bl + ock = _______________ 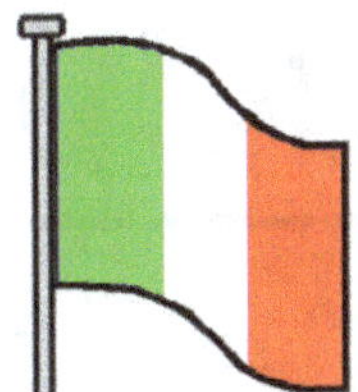

2 cr + ash = _______________

3 fl + ag = _______________ 

4 br + ick = _______________ 

5 cl + iff = _______________

6 fr + ee = _______________ 

New Words

Tracks 10-19

Track
16

bl

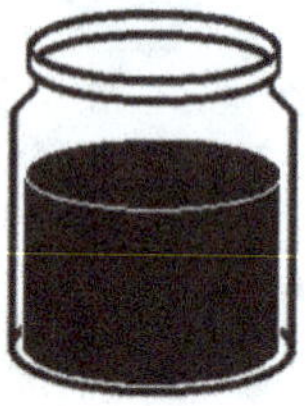

black 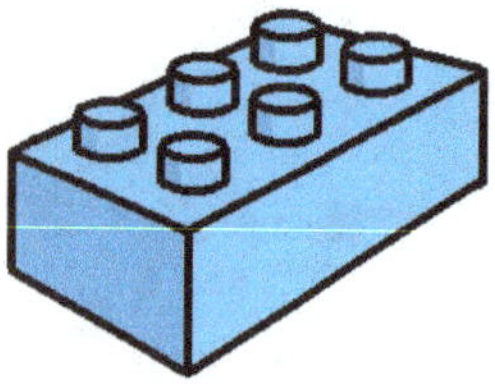   **block**

br

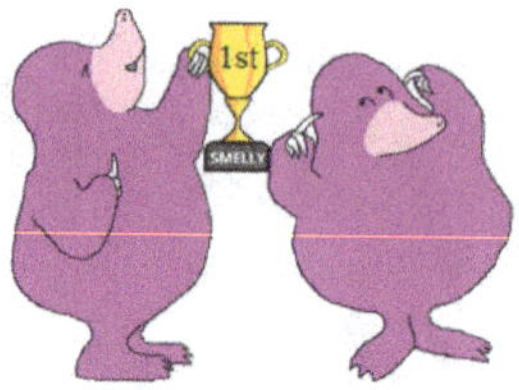

brag 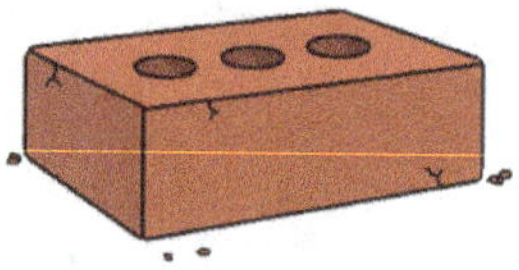   **brick**

cl

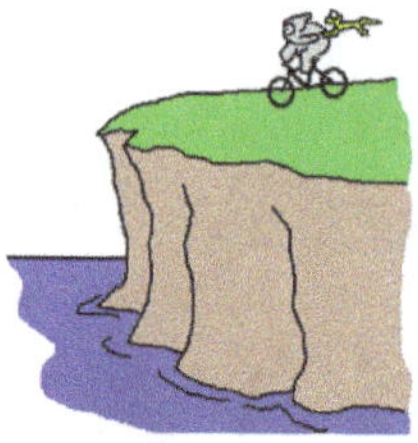

cliff 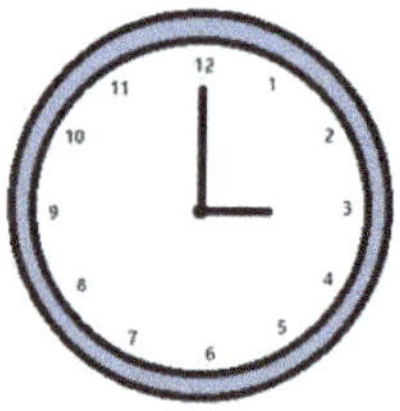   **clock**

cr

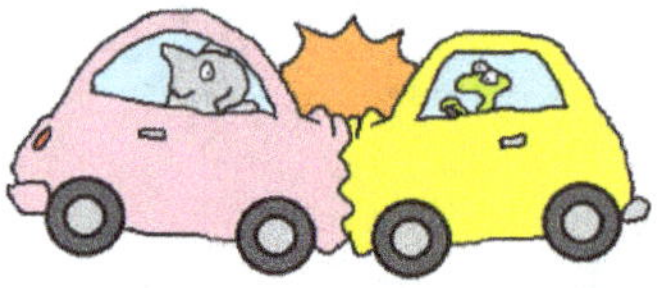

crash 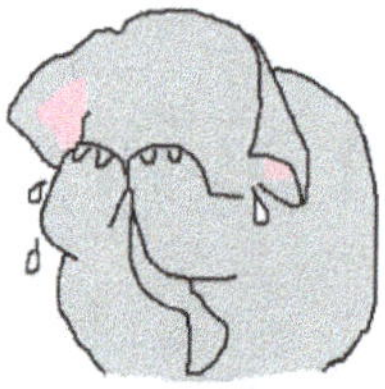   **cry**

fl

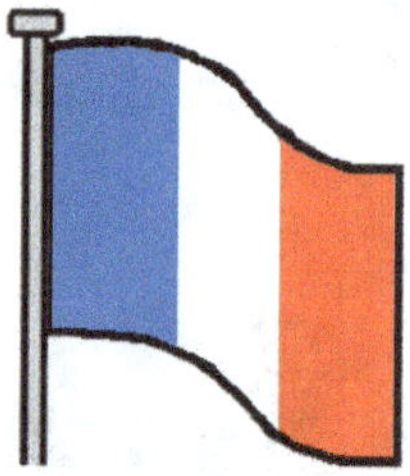

flag 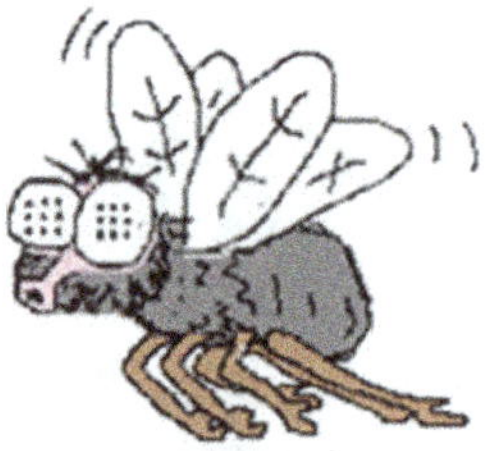   **fly**

fr

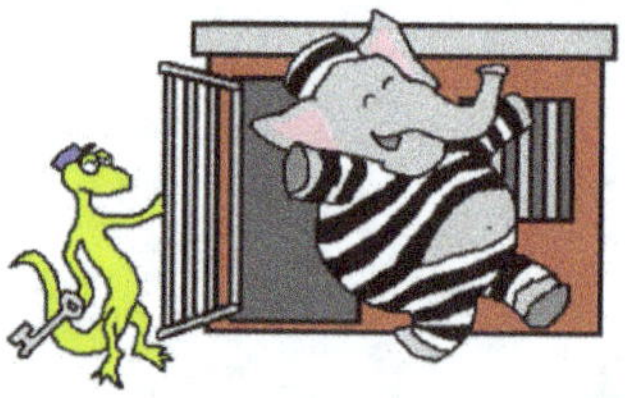

free 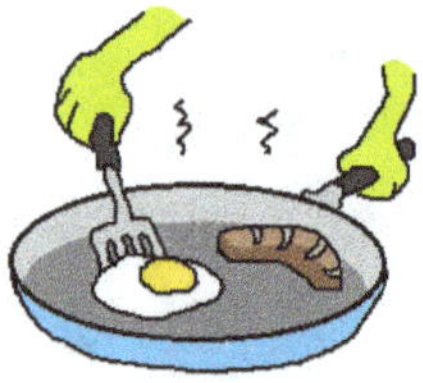   **fry**

Exercises

Listen and write the word

1  _____________

2  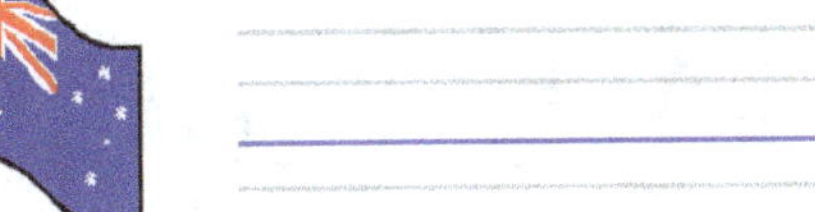 _____________

3 _____________

4 _____________

5  _____________

6 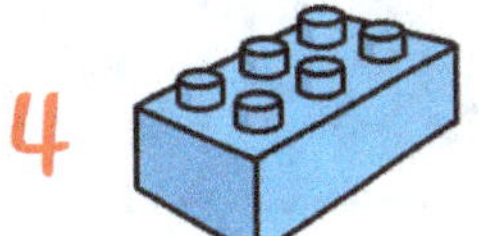 _____________

7  _____________

8  _____________

9  _____________

10  _____________

11  _____________

12  _____________

Listen and circle the right letters AND picture

1 bl cl fl 

2 bl cr fl   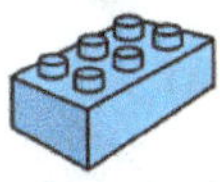 

3 br cl fl   

4 br cr fr   

5 bl cr fr   

6 br cl fr   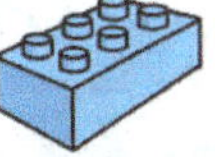  

Circle the word you hear

Circle the sound you hear

1	cl	fr	br	2	bl	fr	cr
3	fl	br	cl	4	cr	bl	fl
5	br	cl	fl	6	bl	cr	fr

Chant

Track
21

Fly the flag
Fly the flag
Fly the black flag!

Crash into a cliff

Fry the flag
Fry the flag
Fry the black flag!

Story

look   T. rex   everyone   come   from

Listen, point, and make the sound:  Words with **gl gr pl pr sl dr**

Tracks 20-29

Track 23

1   g + l = gl

2   d + r = dr

3   p + l = pl

Listen, point, and say the word: Track 24

1   gl + ove = glove 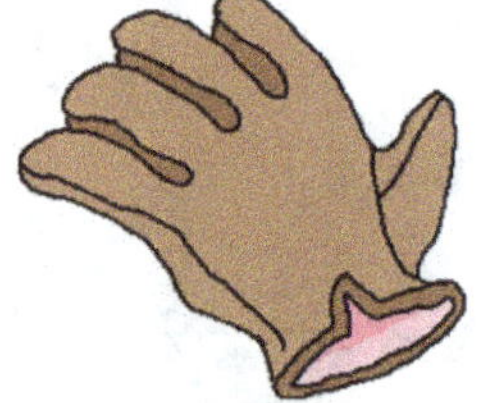

2   dr + ive = drive 

3   pl + um = plum 

Follow the rules

1. gl + ove = __________ 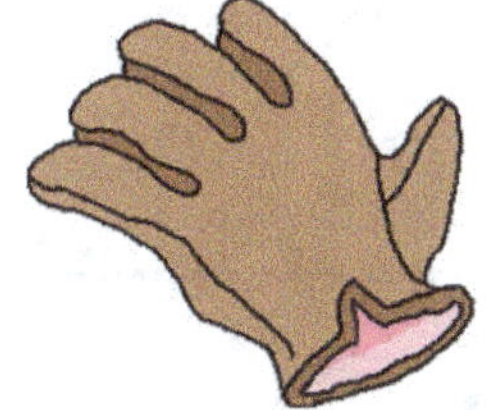

2. dr + ive = __________ 

3. pl + um = __________ 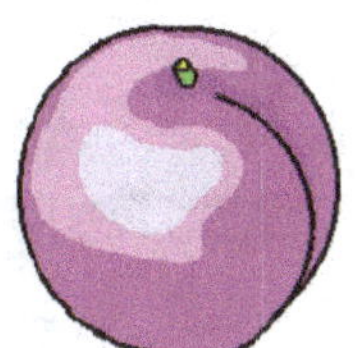

4. sl + ed = __________ 

5. gr + een = __________ 

6. pr + ess = __________ 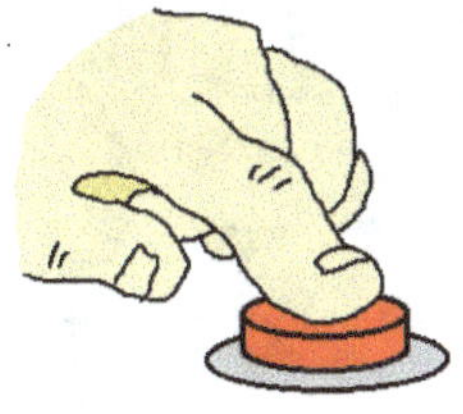

New Words

Listen, point and repeat the new words

Track
25

gl

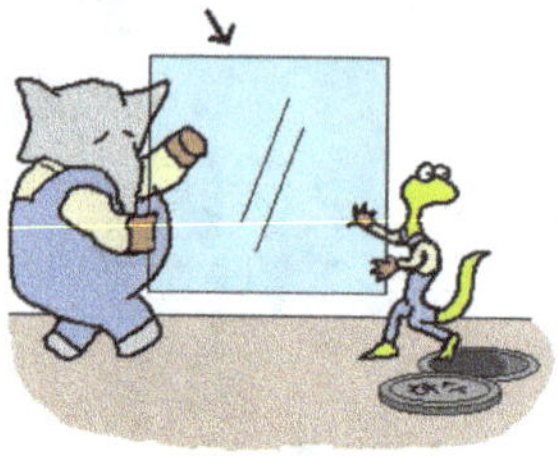

glass 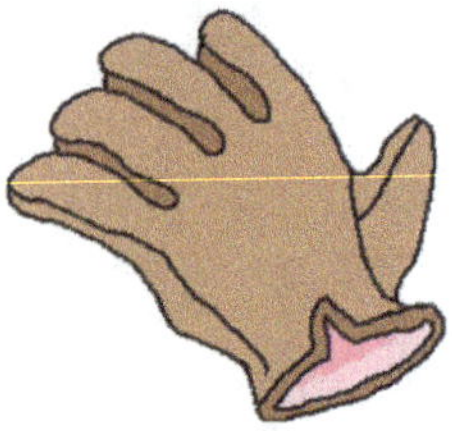 glove

gr

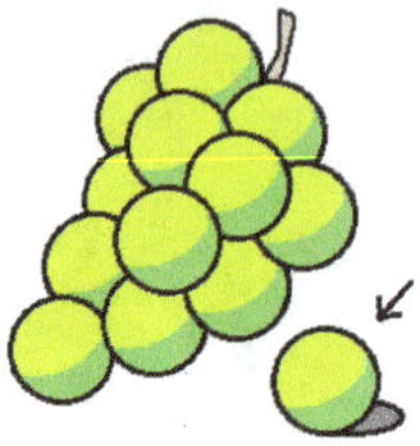

grape 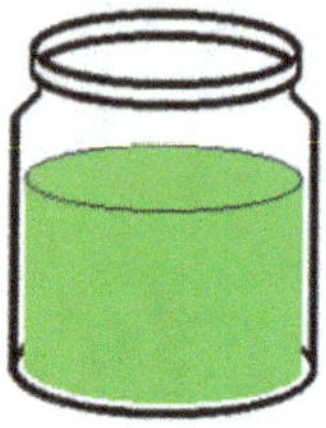 green

pl

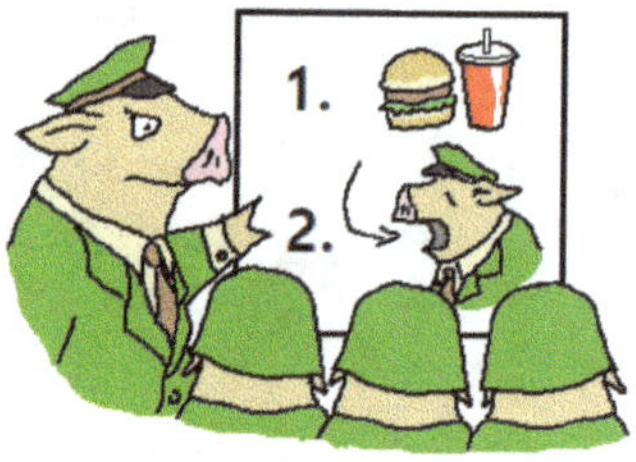

plan 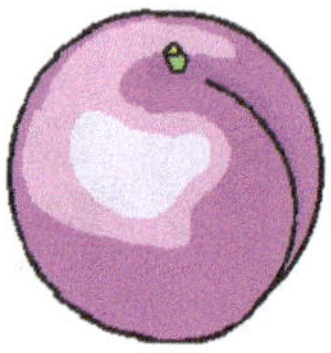 plum

pr

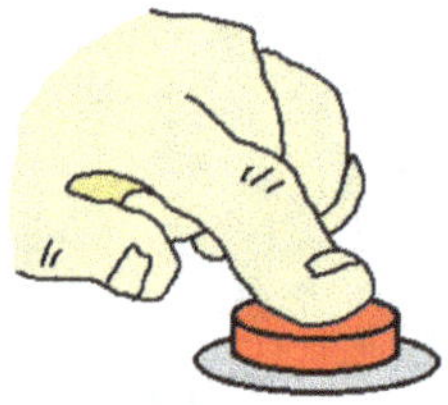

press 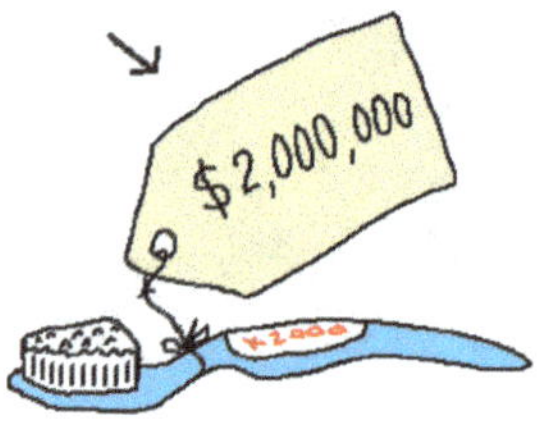 price

dr

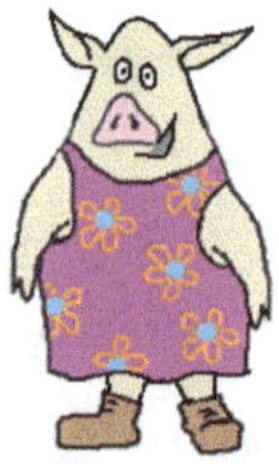

dress 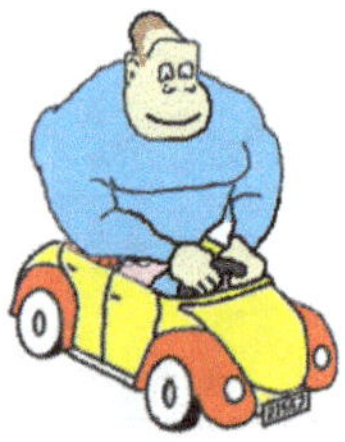 drive

sl

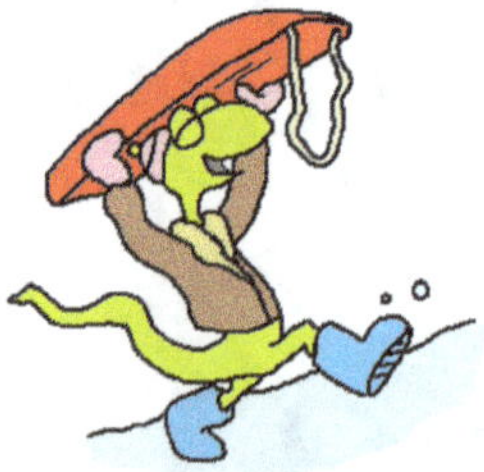

sled 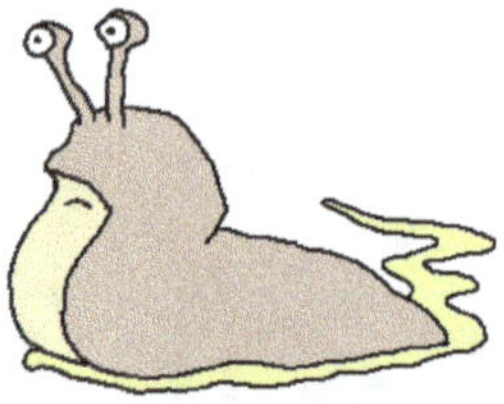 slug

Exercises

Listen and write the word

1  _______________

2  _______________

3  _______________

4  _______________

5  _______________

6  _______________

7  _______________

8  _______________

9 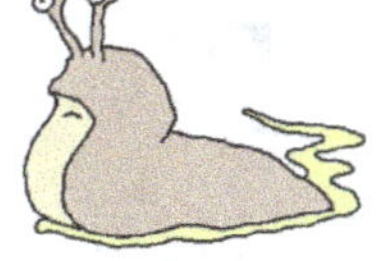 _______________

10 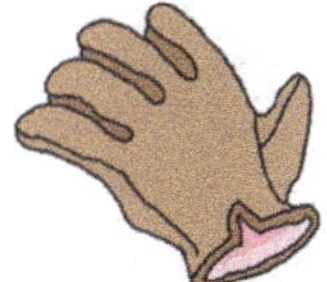 _______________

11  _______________

12  _______________

Listen and circle the right letters AND picture

1 pl gr sl 

2 gl pl sl 

3 dr gr gl 

4 gr pr dr 

5 sl pr dr 

6 pl pr gl 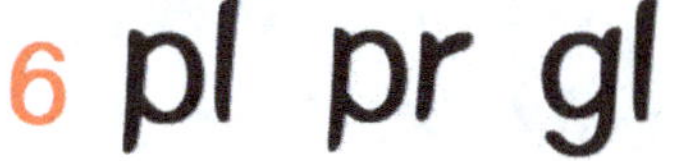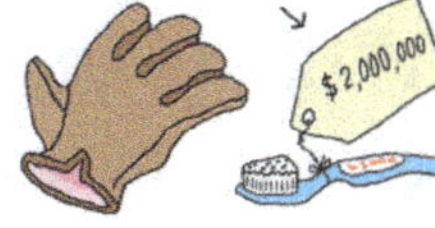

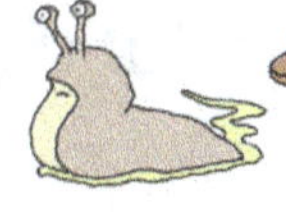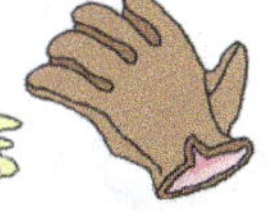

Unit 2   19

Exercises

Circle the word you hear

Tracks 20-29

Track 28

Circle the sound you hear

Track 29

1. dr   gl   pr
2. sl   gr   pl
3. pr   gr   pl
4. dr   gl   sl
5. sl   dr   pl
6. gl   gr   pr

Chant

Sight words: onto

Green dress and gloves!
Green dress and gloves!
Press your face onto the glass
Green dress and gloves!

Green dress and gloves!
Green dress and gloves!
What's the price? What's the price?
Green dress and gloves!

Track 30

Story

Track 31
Tracks 30-39

New Words: sir   move   make   some   slime   slide   later   ready

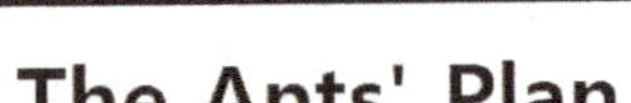

The Ants' Plan

More Sounds

The Story of Q and U

Tracks 20-29

Q and U are married! They are very different. Everyone at the wedding thought a vowel and a consonant were too different to get married, but they didn't care!

U is very outgoing. He often goes out without Q, but Q almost never goes anywhere without U.

Q is almost always with U. When they are together, U is silent. They are very happy together.

More Sounds

Blends are everywhere!

Some blends can start words and some can end them, and some can do both!

And some just sit in the middle!

G is a prankster

When **N** and **G** are together,
G pinches **N**'s nose!
N can't make its usual sound.

So **N** covers **G**'s mouth so it can't say anything at all!

Just sometimes if they are together in the middle of a word **G** can make a sound, though.

Listen and practice the "ng" sound:

 **1** ang  **2** eng  **3** ing  **4** ong  **5** ung

UNIT 3   Consonant Blends

Listen, point, and make the sound:  Words with **-ld -lt -nd -ng -nk -nt**

Tracks 30-39

Track 36

1 n + t = nt

2 n + k = nk

3 n + g = ng

Listen, point, and say the word: Track 37

1 hu + nt = hunt

2 ta + nk = tank

3 ki + ng = king

Write the words

1 hu + nt = ___________ 

2 ta + nk = ___________ 

3 ki + ng = ___________ 

4 ha + nd = ___________ 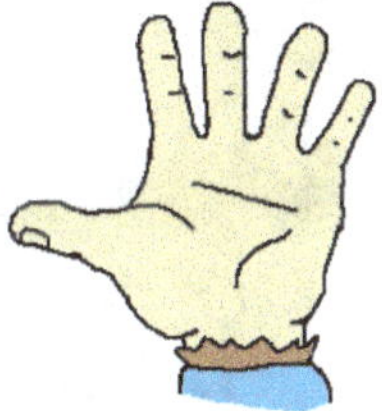

5 qui + lt = ___________ 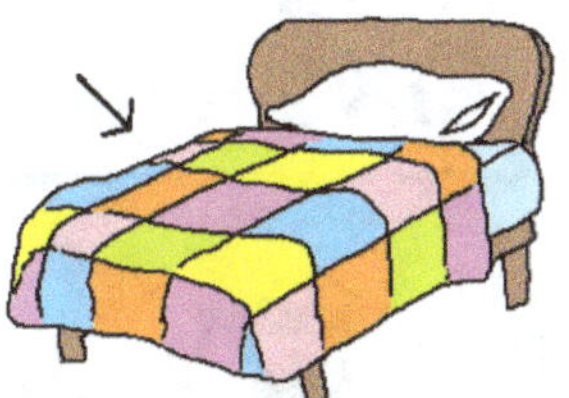

6 co + ld = ___________ 

New Words

Listen, point and repeat the new words

Track 38

-ld

cold   wild

-lt

melt   quilt

-nd

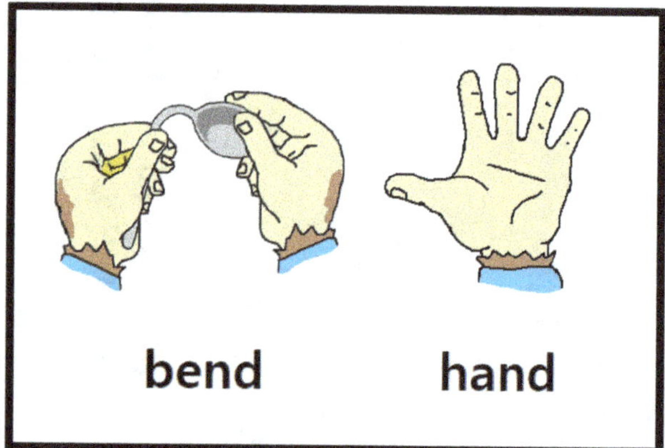

bend   hand

-ng

king   long

-nk

tank   think

-nt

hunt   plant

Exercises

Listen and write the word

1  _______________

2  _______________

3 _______________

4 _______________

5  _______________

6 _______________

7 _______________

8 _______________

9  _______________

10 _______________

11  _______________

12 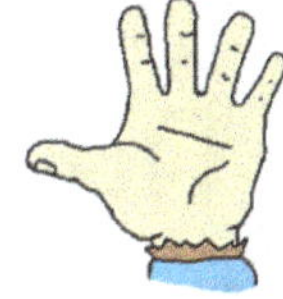 _______________

Listen and circle the right letters AND picture

1 -nt -nk -nd 

2 -ld -nk -ng 

3 -nt -lt -ng 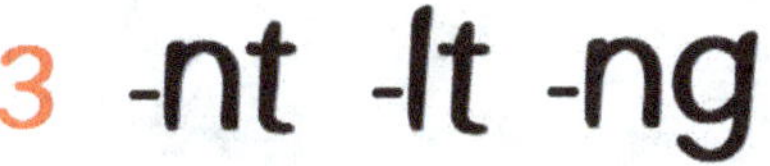

4 -nd -nk -ld 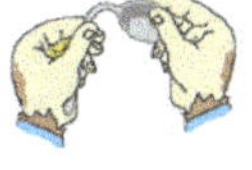

5 -nd -lt -nt 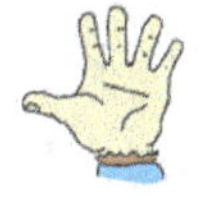

6 -ng -ld -lt 

Exercises

Circle the word you hear

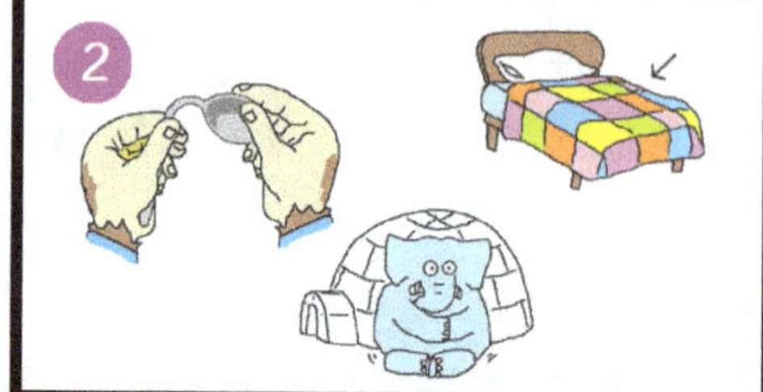

Circle the sound you hear

1. ng   ld   nt
2. nk   nd   lt
3. nd   ng   lt
4. nt   ld   nk
5. nk   nt   lt
6. ld   ng   nd

Chant

New words: glue

Hunt hunt the wild wild plant
Put it in the zoo

A tank for the hunt
A quilt for the cold
A hat and gloves too

Hunt hunt the wild wild plant
Maybe I need glue

Story

Sight words: thing   again

A Thing for the King

Review

Listen and repeat all the words

Review

1. _______________

2. _______________

3. _______________

4. _______________

5. _______________

6. _______________

7. _______________

8. _______________

9. _______________

10. _______________

11. _______________

12. _______________

13. _______________

14. _______________

15. _______________

16. _______________

17. _______________

18. _______________

Review

Find the path

bl br cl cr fl fr gl gr pl pr sl dr -nt -nd -nk -ng -lt -ld

bl br cl cr fl fr gl gr pl pr sl dr -nt -nd -nk -ng -lt -ld

Listen and circle the right word

Track 46

Tracks 40-49

Review

Listen and circle. Then write the number in the word list.

Track 47

Tracks 40-49

1

2

3

4

5

6

7

8

9

10

wild	☐	plum	☐
quilt	☐	think	☐
flag	☐	glass	☐
green	☐	free	☐
black	☐	press	☐

When you finish the last one, sing: "It's a potato.." until the teacher gets angry.

Review   **33**

The Story of the Schwa

Tracks 40-49

Track 48

Consonants

The schwa is a cute little vowel that some letters like as a pet. It makes a sudden noise like dogs do, but it doesn't bark. It sounds like half the u sound.

When we say the consonants' sounds all by themselves, we can hear that some like to have a schwa and some don't.

L,M,N,Q,R,W and Y might sometimes have a tiny little schwa, but it's not really needed. It's more like an accessory. We all know pets shouldn't be accessories, so we try not to give them a schwa.

Track 49

Any consonant can have a schwa, but most shouldn't. B,D,G and J can't help but have one.

Track 50

: **BDGJ**

: **CFHKPSTVXZ**

: **LMNQRWY**

Even More Sounds

The Story of the Schwa

Vowels

If a vowel has a pet schwa
it feels a bit uncomfortable
because the schwa will always
drown out its sound.

Tracks 50-59

The schwa looks like an
upside-down **e**, but we
never write it.
It's not allowed to be
written in a word!

Consonant blends and the schwa

Track 52

You might hear a little schwa
in some blends, but never in
the ones that have no voice.
They don't like it. Perhaps
those blends are a little bit
difficult to say.

Track 53

Try to say some of the difficult ones with your teacher:

1 sp 2 st 3 sk 4 sc 5 cht 6 sht

UNIT 4   Consonant Blends

Listen, point, and make the sound:  Words with **ph ch sh -ph -ch -sh**

Tracks 50-59

Track 54

1 p + h = ph

2 c + h = ch

3 s + h = sh

Listen, point, and say the word: Track 55

1 ph + one = phone 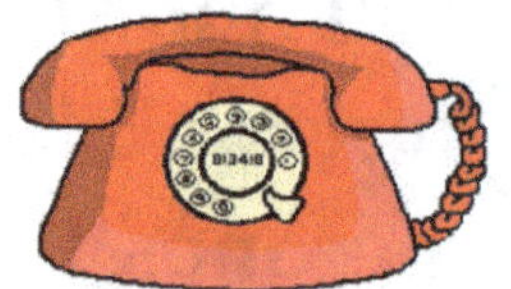

2 ri + ch = rich 

3 sh + ip = ship

Follow the rules

Write the words

1   **ph + one =** __________

2   **ri + <u>ch</u> =** __________

3   **sh + ip =** __________

4   **gra + <u>ph</u> =** __________

5   **ch + in =** __________

6   **pu + <u>sh</u> =** __________

New Words

Tracks 50-59

Listen, point and repeat the new words

ch

chin   chop

-ch

much   rich

ph

phone   photo

-ph

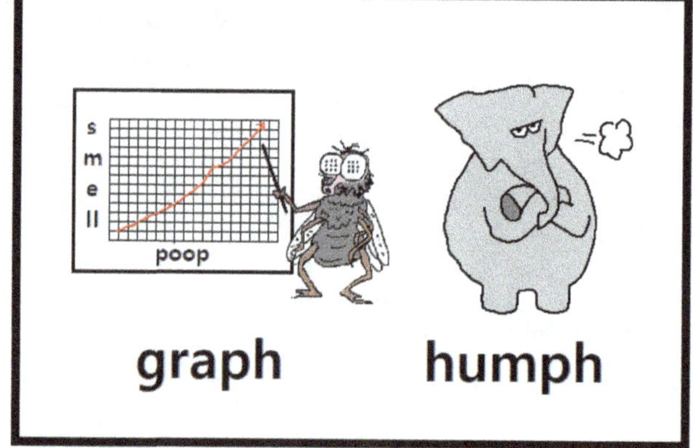

graph   humph

sh

shake   ship

-sh

cash   push

Exercises

Listen and write the word

Tracks 50-59

1  ________________

2  ________________

3  ________________

4  ________________

5  ________________

6  ________________

7  ________________

8 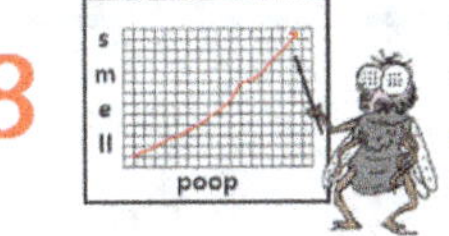 ________________

9  ________________

10  ________________

11  ________________

12  ________________

Listen and circle the right letters AND picture

1 sh -ch ph 

2 sh -ch ph  

3 -sh ch -ph   

4 -sh ch -ph   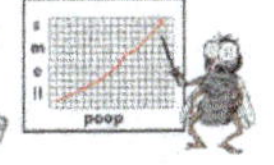

5 -sh ch -ph   

6 sh -ch ph  

Exercises

Circle the word you hear

Track 59

Tracks 50-59

Circle the sound you hear

Track 60

1. sh   ch   ph   2. sh   ch   ph

3. sh   ch   ph   4. sh   ch   ph

5. sh   ch   ph   6. sh   ch   ph

Chant

Track 61   Sight words: check

Rich man on his ship
How much? How much?
Check the graph!

Rich man on the phone
How much? How much?
Check the cash!

Listen and read along

Sight words: very just should whole wow

Chin Man

Humph! That ship is not huge.

UNIT 5   Consonant Blends

Listen, point, and make the sound:  Words with **th sp sm -th -sp tr**

Tracks 60-69

Track 63

1   t + h = th

2   s + p = sp

3   t + r = tr

Listen, point, and say the word: Track 64

1   th + ick = thick

2   wa + sp = wasp

3   tr + uck = truck

Write the words

1 th + ick = __________ 

2 wa + sp = __________ 

3 tr + uck = __________ 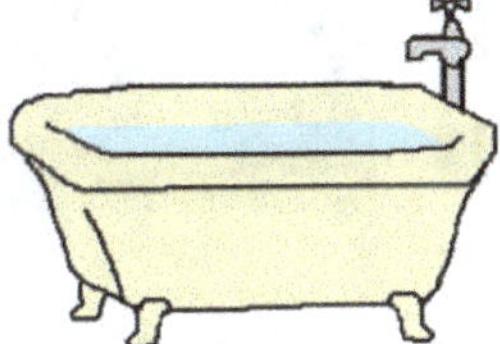

4 ba + th = __________ 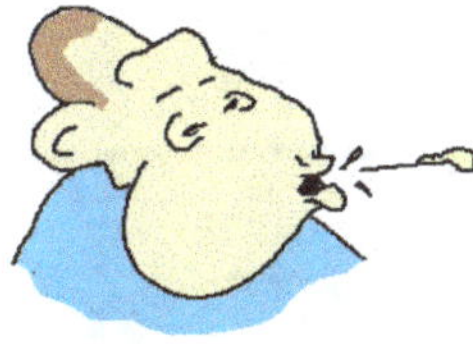

5 sp + it = __________

6 sm + oke = __________ 

New Words

Tracks 60-69

Listen, point and repeat the new words

Track 65

th

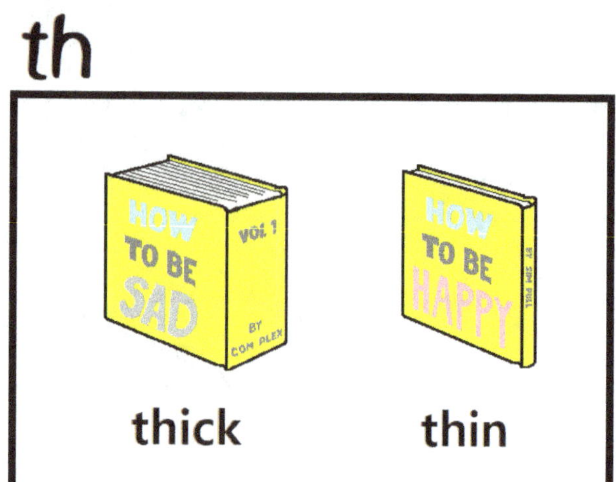

thick   thin

-th

bath   moth

sp

space   spit

-sp

gasp   wasp

sm

smile   smoke

tr

trash   truck

Exercises

Listen and write the word

1 

2  

3 ________

4 ________

5  

6 ________

7 

8  

9 

10  

11 

12 

Listen and circle the right letters AND picture

1 sp sm th 

2 sp tr th 

3 -sp sm -th   

4 -sp tr -th   

5 -sp sm -th  

6 sp tr th  

Exercises

Circle the word you hear

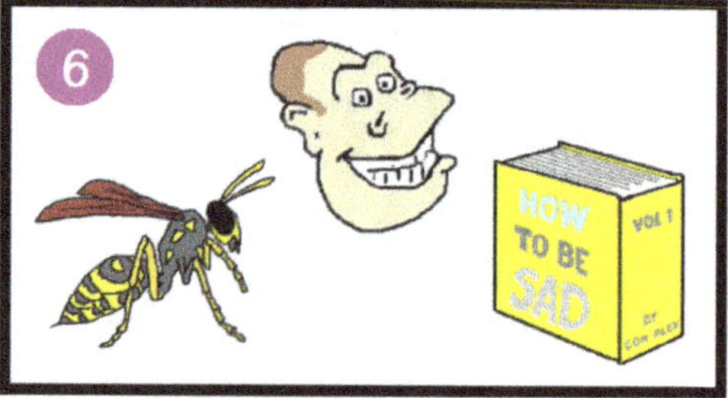

Circle the sound you hear

1	sp	sm	th	2	sp	tr	th
3	sp	tr	th	4	sp	sm	th
5	sp	sm	th	6	sp	tr	th

Chant

Sight words: choke

Trash truck in the thick black smoke
Trash truck in the thick black smoke
Choke and spit and gasp

Trash truck in the thick black smoke
Trash truck in the thick black smoke
I think I need a bath

Story

Track 71

Tracks 70-79

New sight words: aim suit smash

Space Wasp vs. Moth Man 	**Moth Man fixes his spaceship.** 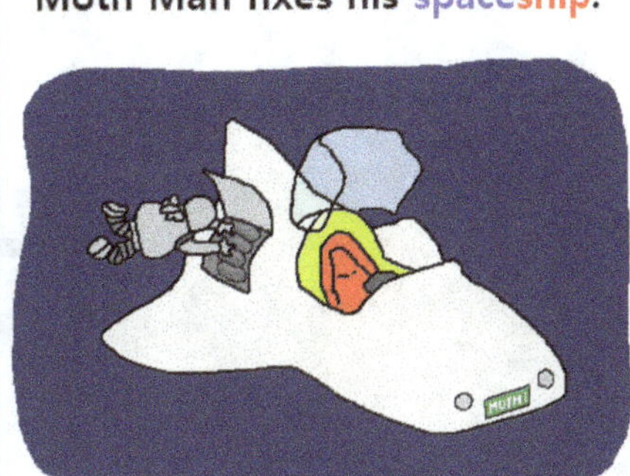	**But Space Wasp can see him.** 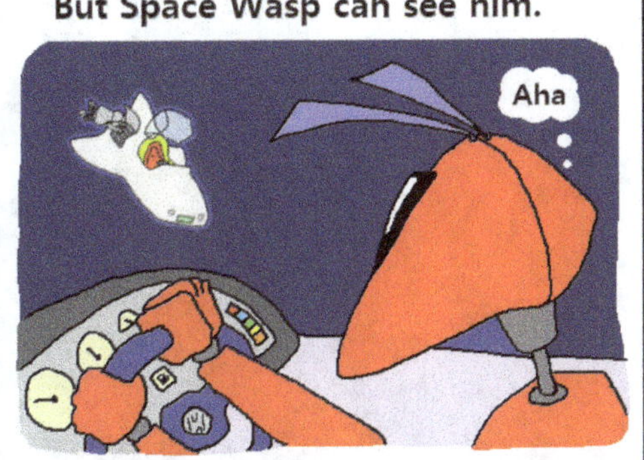
Space Wasp has a scary spaceship. 	**Space Wasp aims at Moth Man.** 	**Moth Man has no time to think!** 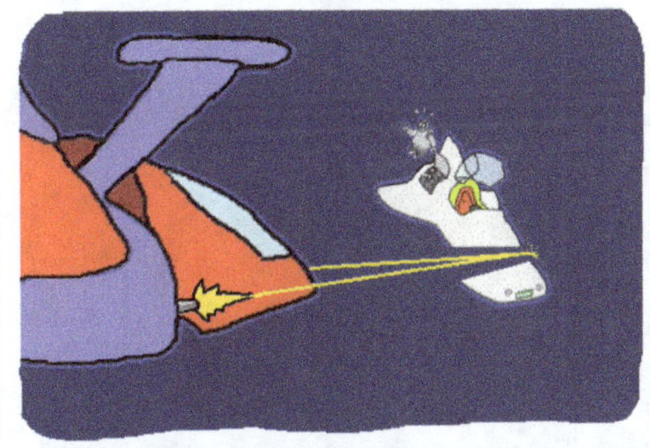
Space Wasp's ship cuts a thin line. 	**But the space suit is too thick!** 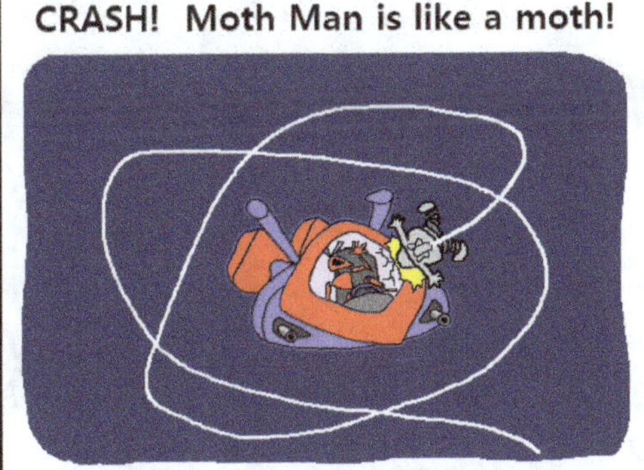	**CRASH! Moth Man is like a moth!** 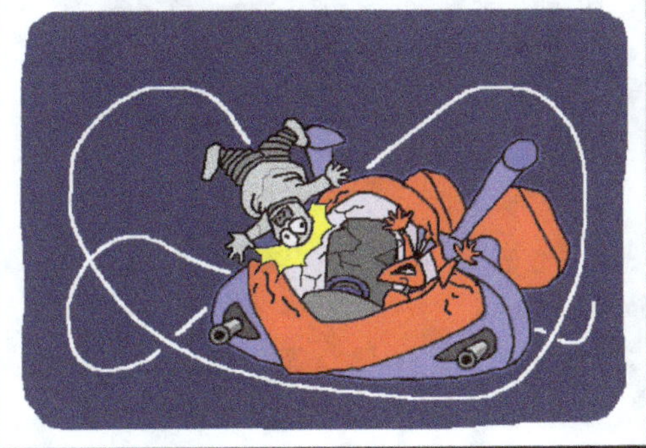
Space Wasp says, "I give up!" 	**Space Wasp's ship is smashed!** 	**And Moth Man smiles!**

Listen, point, and make the sound: 

Words with **st sk sc sn**
-st -sk -sc sw

Tracks 70-79

Track 72

1   s + t = st

2   s + k = sk

3   s + n = sn

Listen, point, and say the word:

Track 73

1   st + op = stop

2   ma + sk = mask

3   sn + ake = snake

Follow the rules

Write the words

1   st + op = __________   

2   ma + sk = __________   

3   sn + ake = __________   

4   ve + st = __________   

5   sc + uba = __________   

6   sw + im = __________   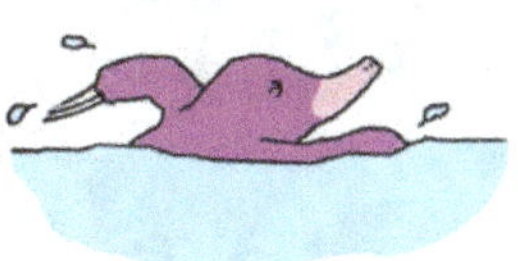

New Words

Tracks 70-79

Listen, point and repeat the new words

Track 74

st

stop · strong

-st

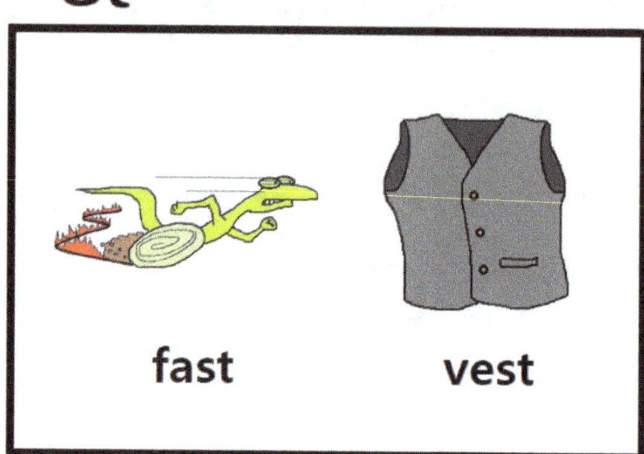

fast · vest

sc/sk

scuba · sky

-sc/-sk

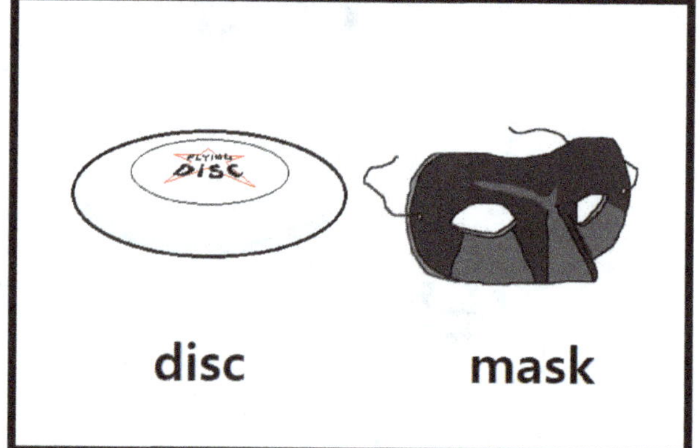

disc · mask

sn

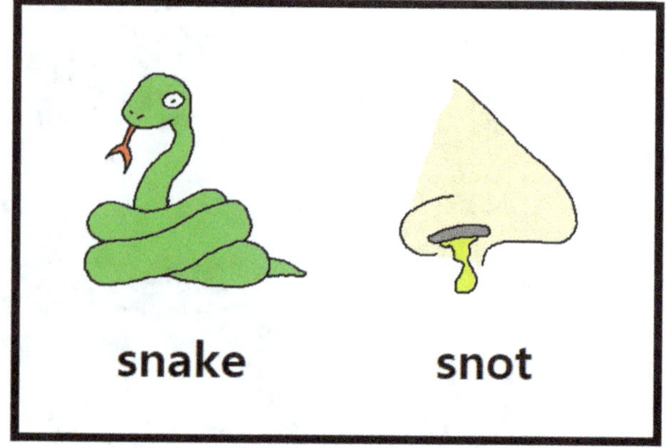

snake · snot

sw

swan · swim

Exercises

Listen and write the word

1  __________

2 __________

3 __________

4 __________

5  __________ 6  __________

7  __________ 8  __________

9  __________ 10 __________

11  __________ 12  __________

Listen and circle the right letters AND picture

1 st sn sk  

2 st sw sc 

3 -st sn -sk 

4 -st sw -sk 

5 -st sn -sc  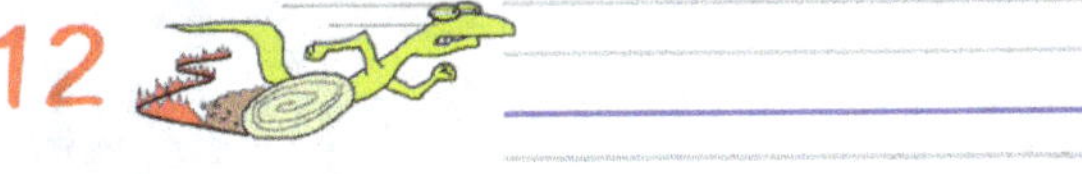

6 st sw sc 

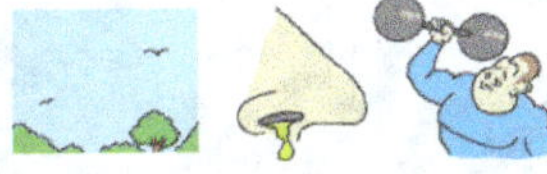

Exercises

Circle the word you hear

Tracks 70-79

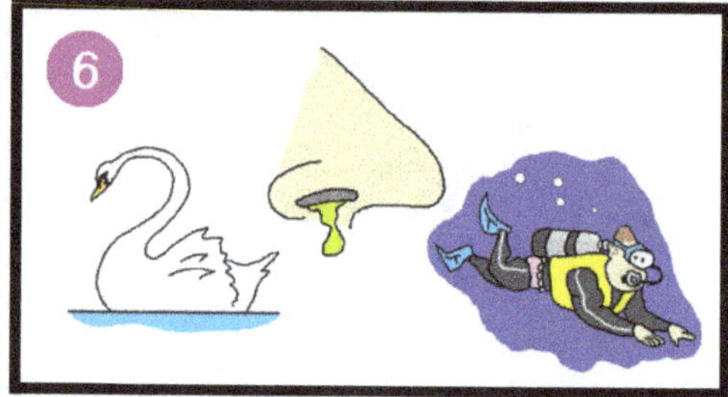

Circle the sound you hear

1. st   sn   sk   2. st   sw   sk

3. st   sw   sc   4. st   sn   sc

5. st   sn   sk   6. st   sw   sc

Chant

Sight words: as

Snake in a scuba mask
Swimming in the sea
Strong and fast
As he can be

Swan in a scuba mask
Swimming in the sea
Strong and fast
As he can be

Story

Listen and read along

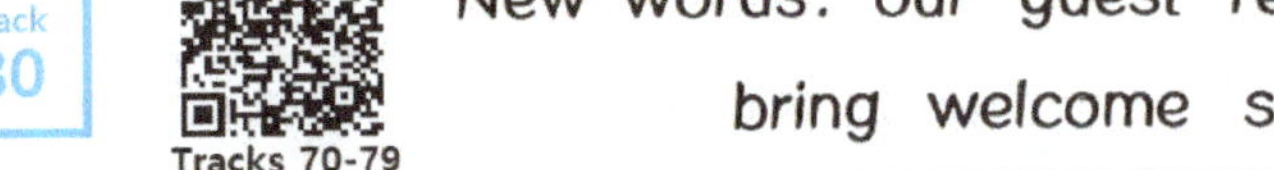

New words: our guest really bring welcome sorry sneeze

Review

Track 81

Tracks 80-89

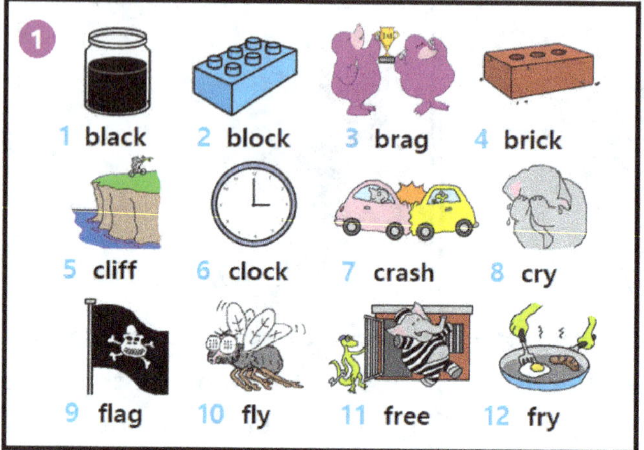

1
1 black
2 block
3 brag
4 brick
5 cliff
6 clock
7 crash
8 cry
9 flag
10 fly
11 free
12 fry

2
1 glass
2 glove
3 grape
4 green
5 plan
6 plum
7 press
8 price
9 dress
10 drive
11 sled
12 slug

3
1 cold
2 wild
3 melt
4 quilt
5 bend
6 hand
7 king
8 long
9 tank
10 think
11 hunt
12 plant

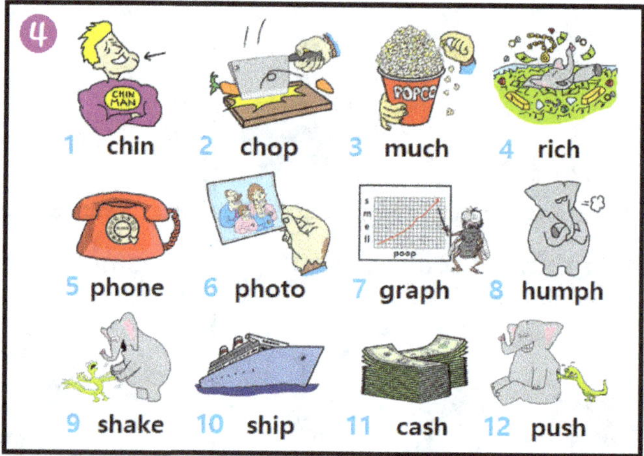

4
1 chin
2 chop
3 much
4 rich
5 phone
6 photo
7 graph
8 humph
9 shake
10 ship
11 cash
12 push

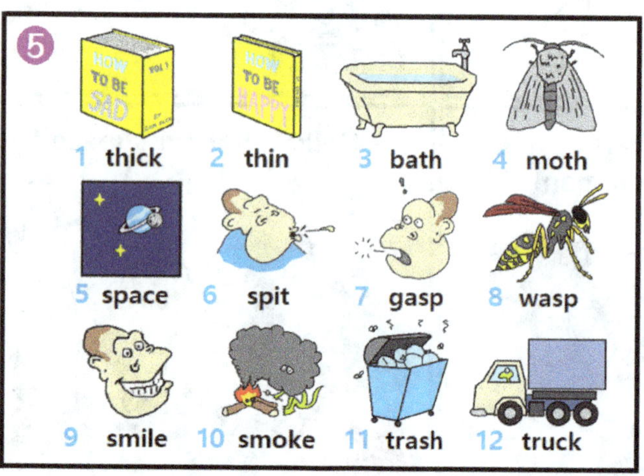

5
1 thick
2 thin
3 bath
4 moth
5 space
6 spit
7 gasp
8 wasp
9 smile
10 smoke
11 trash
12 truck

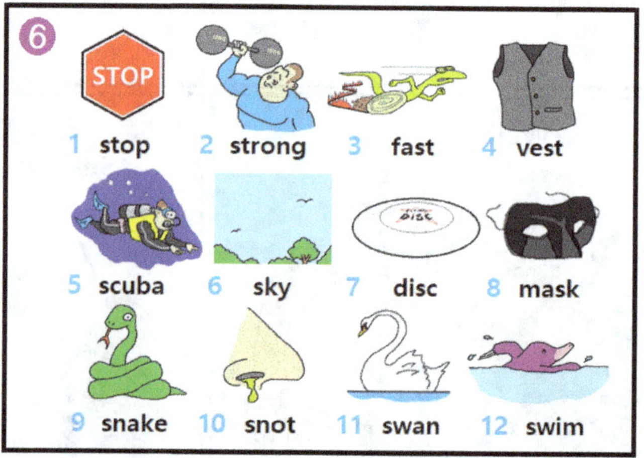

6
1 stop
2 strong
3 fast
4 vest
5 scuba
6 sky
7 disc
8 mask
9 snake
10 snot
11 swan
12 swim

Review

Say the word and write it

1		2	
3		4	
5		6	
7		8	
9		10	
11		12	
13		14	
15		16	
17		18	

Find the path

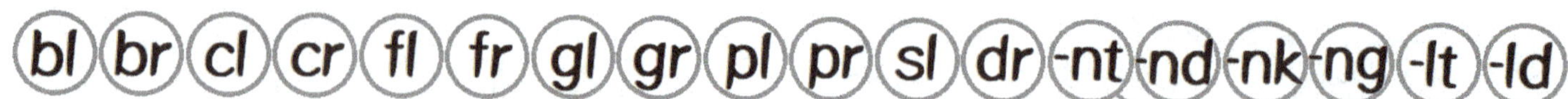

bl br cl cr fl fr gl gr pl pr sl dr -nt -nd -nk -ng -lt -ld

bl br cl cr fl fr gl gr pl pr sl dr -nt -nd -nk -ng -lt -ld

Find the path again

ph -ph ch -ch sh -sh th -th sp -sp sm tr st -st sk -sc sn sw

ph -ph ch -ch sh -sh th -th sp -sp sm tr st -st sc -sk sn sw

Review

Listen and circle. Then write the number in the word list.

Tracks 80-89

Track 82

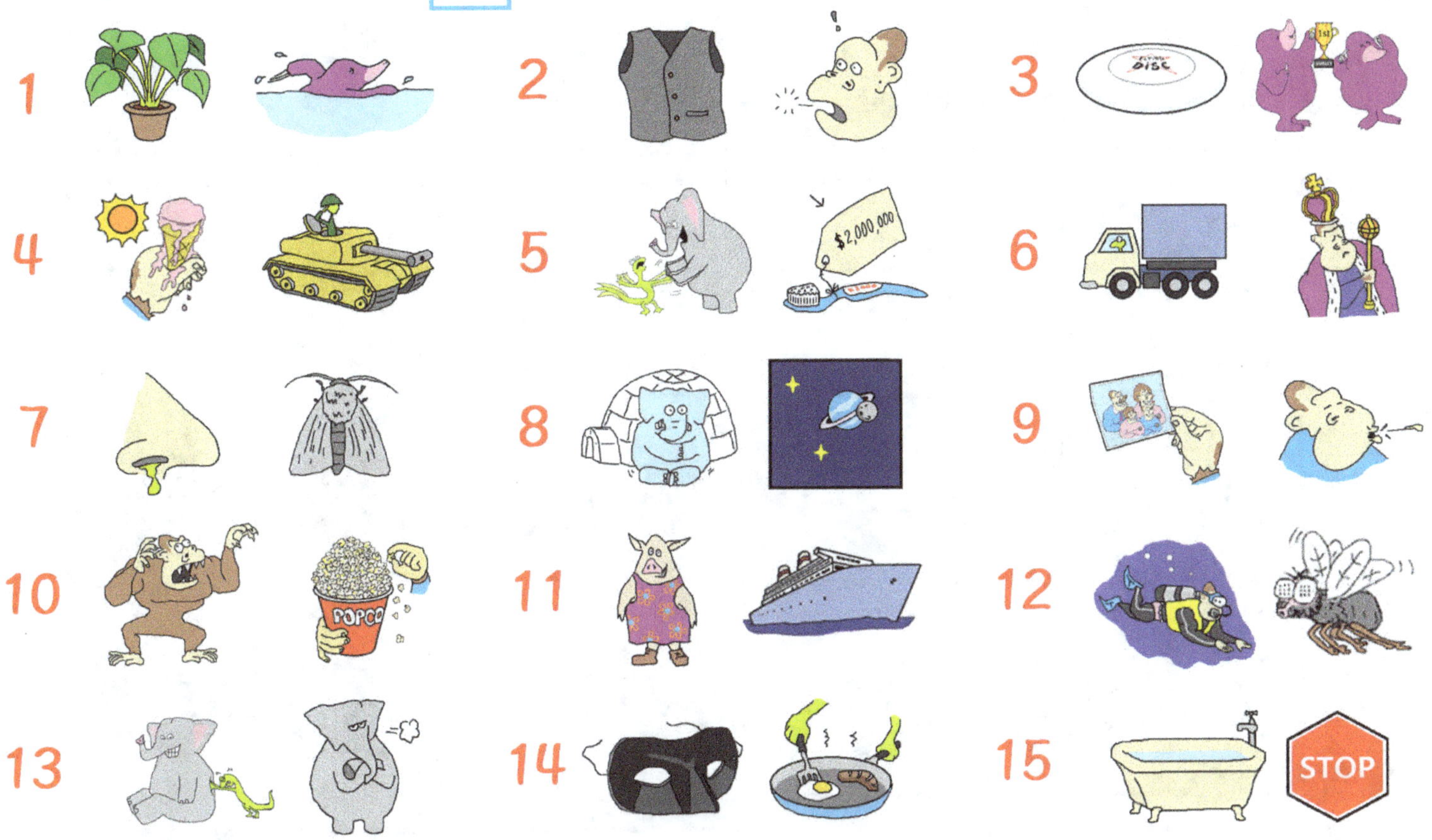

1   2   3

4   5   6

7   8   9

10   11   12

13   14   15

brag ☐	mask ☐	plant ☐
scuba ☐	vest ☐	space ☐
melt ☐	ship ☐	push ☐
wild ☐	king ☐	bath ☐
snot ☐	price ☐	photo ☐

When you finish the last one, cluck like a chicken and don't stop until the teacher says:

"Okay, okay, I'm smelly."

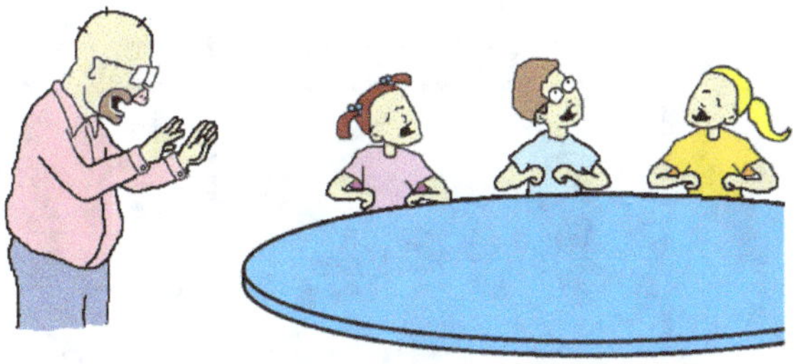

Test

Listen and circle

a  Track 83 b  Track 84 c  Track 85

1        

2    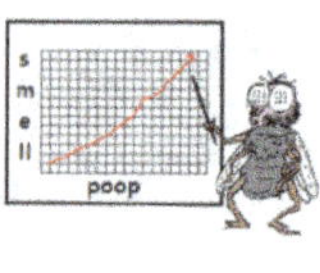   

3   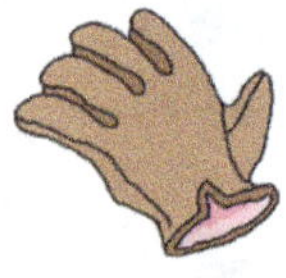    

4     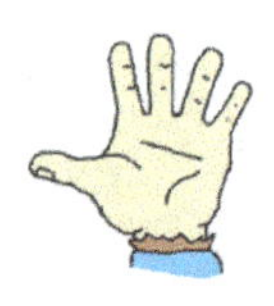  

5       

6       

7       

Test

Listen and write the blend (or digraph)

a Track 86   b Track 87   c Track 88

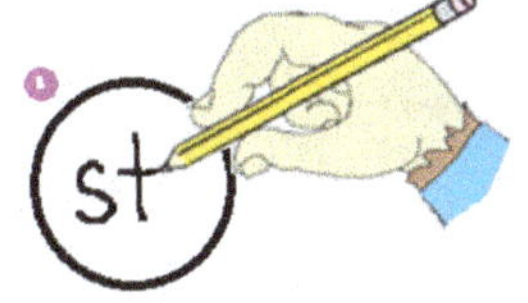

Tracks 80-89

1 ◯ 2 ◯ 3 ◯ 4 ◯

5 ◯ 6 ◯ 7 ◯ 8 ◯

9 ◯ 10 ◯ 11 ◯ 12 ◯

13 ◯ 14 ◯ 15 ◯ 16 ◯

Test

Listen and circle

a | Track 89 | b | Track 90 | c | Track 91

1		sm	dr	th	sw	-nd	-sk
2		tr	-nk	-sp	ph	-ld	cr
3		-ng	sc	ch	br	-lt	-st
4		fr	-ph	sp	st	-nt	pr
5		bl	gr	sh	sl	-ch	fl
6		cl	-sh	pl	-th	gl	sn

Test

Choose a picture and write the word to match

1

2

3

4

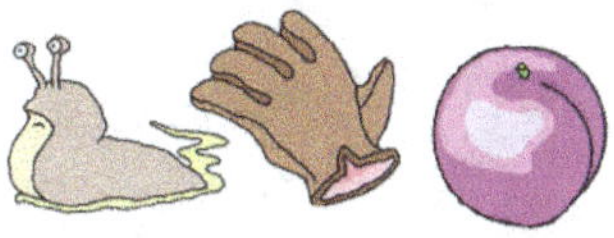

5

6

7

8

9

10

11

12

13

14

15

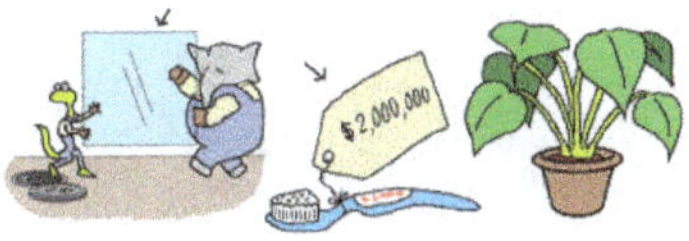

16

17

18

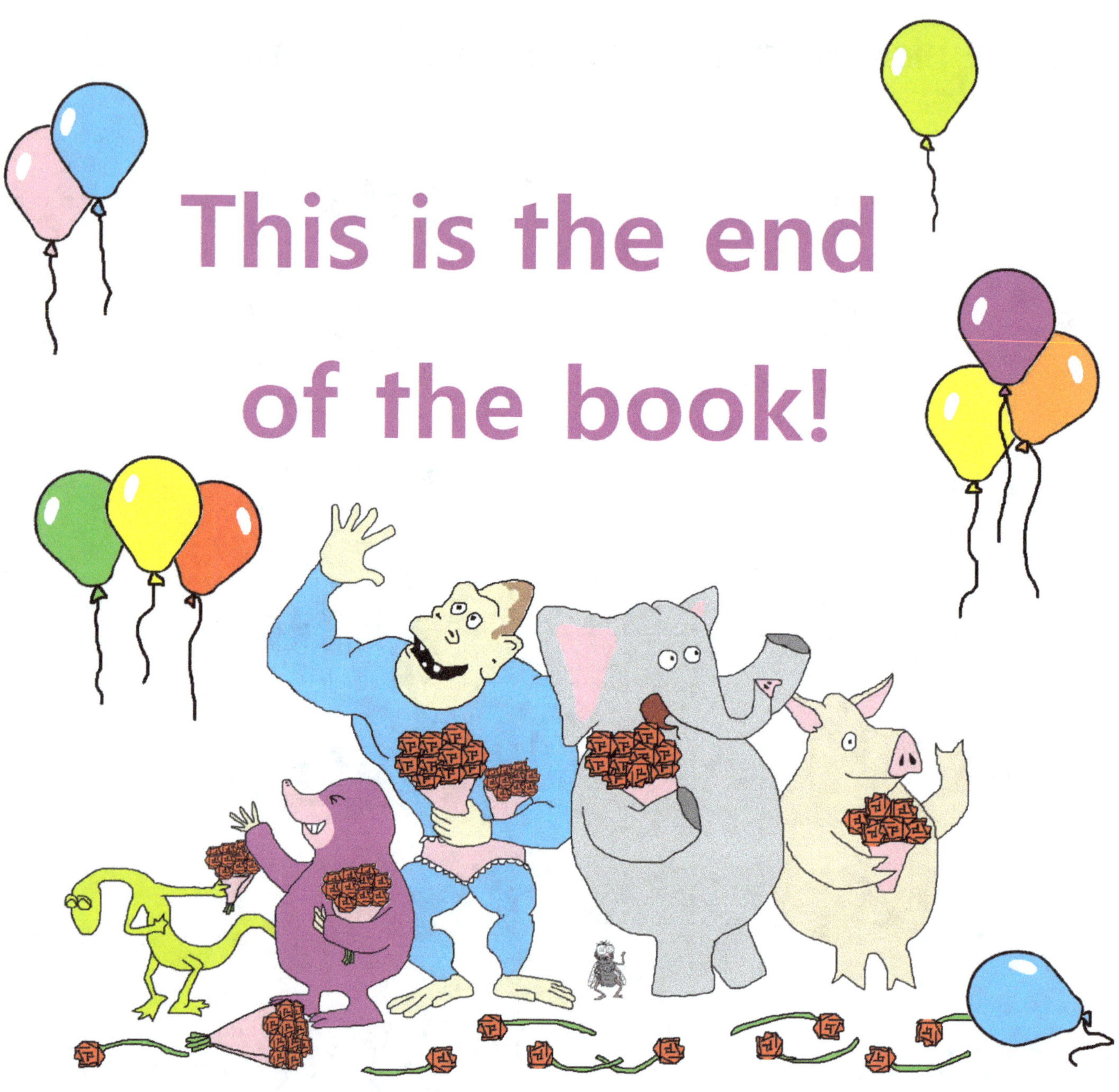

This is the end
of the book!

Word List

Unit 1

black

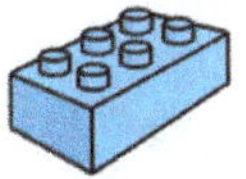
block

brag

brick

cliff

clock

crash

cry

flag

fly

free

fry

Unit 2

glass

glove

grape

green

plan

plum

press

price

dress

drive

sled

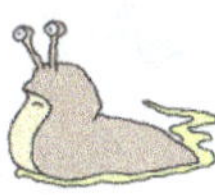
slug

Unit 3

cold

wild

melt

quilt

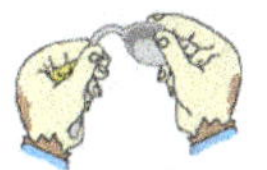
bend

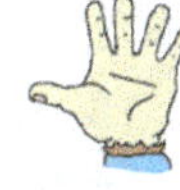
hand

king

long

tank

think

hunt

plant

Word List

Unit 4

chin	chop	much	rich
		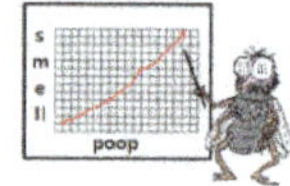	
phone	photo	graph	humph

shake	ship	cash	push

Unit 5

			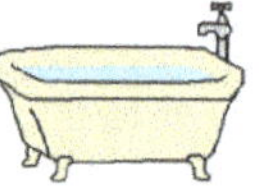
thick	thin	bath	moth

space	spit	gasp	wasp

smile	smoke	trash	truck

Unit 6

stop	strong	fast	vest

scuba	sky	disc	mask

snake	snot	swan	swim

Our Sight Words

Word	Note (ESL)	Word	Note (ESL)
a/an		by	
and		fellow	
all		say	
on		go	
in		to	
the		win	
no		I	
lift		had	
like		it	
get		wait	
oh		have	
not		that	
did		yummy	
you		what	
your		she	
yes		wear	
my		so	
has		scary	
put		will	
one		fell	

Our Sight Words

Word	Note (ESL)	Word	Note (ESL)
down		many	
am/are		with	
want		call	
give		must	
me		now	
him		need	
shut		maybe	
he		don't	
handsome		play	
pretty		take	
let's		us	
okay		first	
talk		brush	
do		bake	
or		with	
cent		this	
stop		we	
see		whose	
too		make	
them		new	

Our Sight Words

Word	Note (ESL)	Word	Note (ESL)
be		lit	
best		people	
can		yell	
leave		his	
at		poem	
but		into	
after		birthday	
even		walk	
next		maid	
hello		never	
for		P15 look	
home		T. rex	
room		everyone	
only		come	
also		from	
can't		P20 onto	
is		sir	
ate		move	
still		make	
soup		some	

Our Sight Words

Word	Note (ESL)	Word	Note (ESL)
slime		really	
slide		bring	
later		welcome	
ready		sorrry	
P28 glue		sneeze	
thing			
again			
P40 check			
very			
just			
should			
whole			
wow			
P46 choke			
aim			
suit			
smash			
P52 as			
our			
guest			

OUR SIGHT WORD FLASH CARDS!

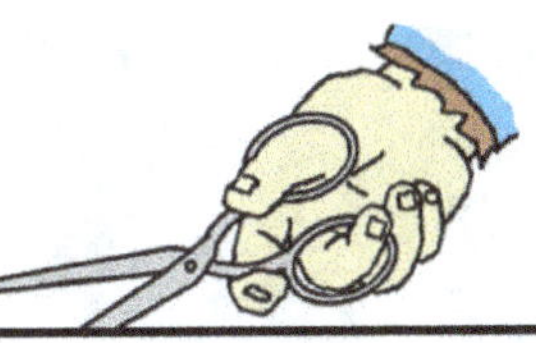

look	T. rex
everyone	**come**
from	**onto**
sir	**move**

OUR SIGHT WORD FLASH CARDS!

some	slime
slide	later
ready	glue
thing	again

OUR SIGHT WORD FLASH CARDS!

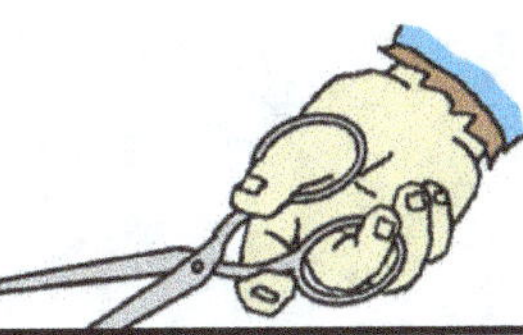

check	very
just	should
whole	wow
choke	aim

suit

smash

as

our

guest

really

bring

welcome

sorry

sneeze

don't

take

with

this

but

also

OUR SIGHT WORD FLASH CARDS!

we	be
his	for
what	too
him	down

see	too
can	will
have	give
are	the

OUR SIGHT WORD FLASH CARDS!

and	has
my	get
your	not
by	to

Phonics Series

Preschool:

Kindergarten:

Elementary School Junior:

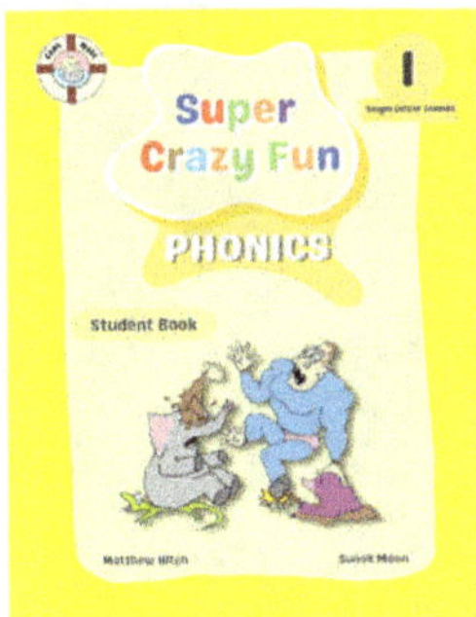 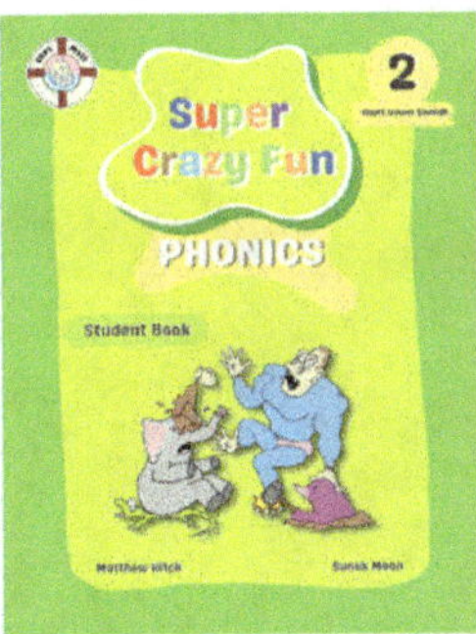 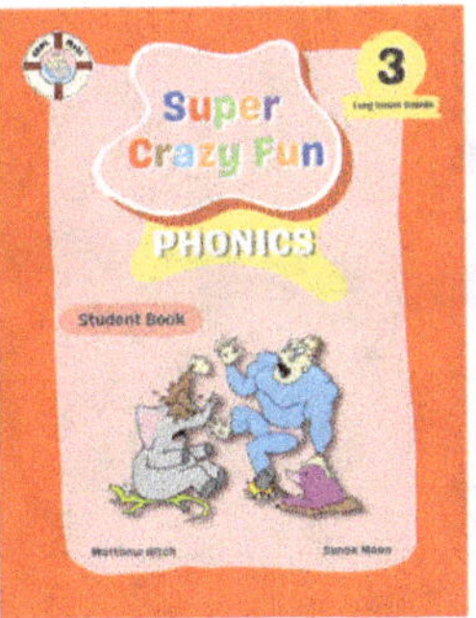  

Elementary School Senior/Remedial:

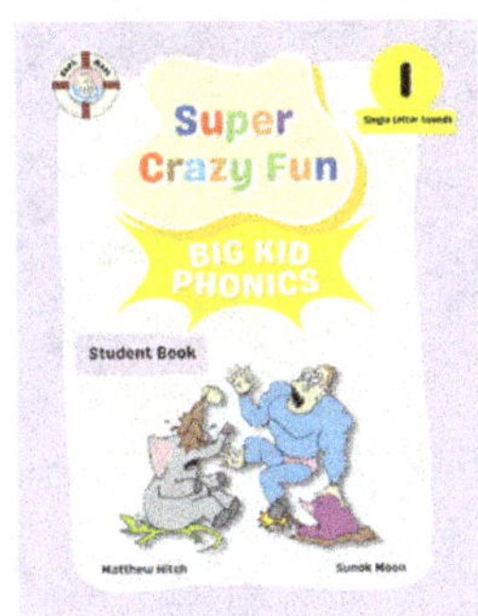 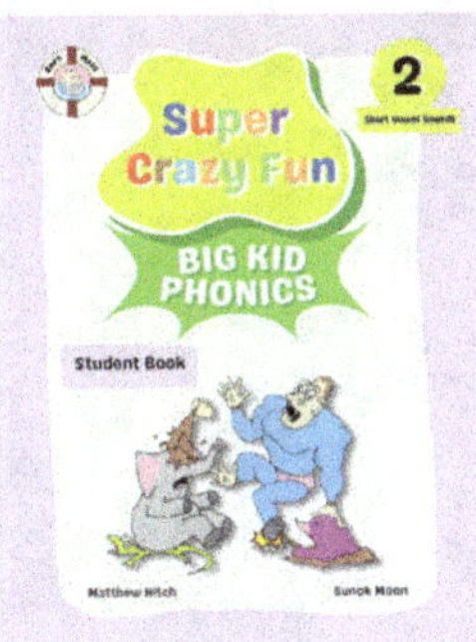   

www.ingramcontent.com/pod-product-compliance
Lightning Source LLC
Chambersburg PA
CBHW080754120726
48001CB00009B/2744